Henry Sibley's
First Years at St. Peters
or Mendota

Henry H. Sibley's house, built a few years after his arrival in Minnesota in 1834, as it looked in March 2002.
BRUCE WHITE PHOTO.

Henry Sibley's
First Years at St. Peters
or Mendota

Helen M. White

Turnstone Historical Research
St. Paul, Minnesota

Edited by Ann Regan and Virginia Martin
Designed by Diane Eagon and Bruce White
Production by Diane Eagon
Set in Garamond
Printed by Sexton Printing

Turnstone Historical Research
St. Paul, Minnesota

ABOUT THE COVER: This view of the mouth of the Minnesota River and Fort Snelling was painted by Edward K. Thomas who as a sergeant in the U.S. Army was stationed at the fort from 1849 to 1851. Thomas painted various versions of this same view. This one, from the Sibley House collection, donated by Eli Pettijohn, may have been similar to the painting described as being in Sibley's possession throughout his life, supposedly showing the area of St. Peters as it was in the 1830s. Although Thomas was not at Fort Snelling at that time, he emphasized details of the scene that were present earlier.

Henry H. Sibley's Place in Minnesota

Minnesota is greatly changed since 1834, when Henry Sibley arrived at St. Peters, or Mendota as it was later called. Yet visitors to Mendota and nearby Fort Snelling today may find much to suggest earlier times. Woods have taken over the valley where the Minnesota and Mississippi come together. The waters still flow pure at nearby springs. At Historic Fort Snelling, guides in period costume re-enact the lives of soldiers and fur traders. Sibley's house and other buildings have been lovingly restored by the Sibley House Association, a group founded by the Daughters of the American Revolution.

The restoration of Sibley's house, which may have been the first effort at historic preservation in Minnesota, was a tribute to Sibley's pivotal role in Minnesota's early years. Sibley arrived in Minnesota as a fur trader, but he transcended a period of rapid change as settlers surged into the territory in the 1840s and 1850s. He then became a successful and respected politician, serving as the state's first governor. He left his name on streets, towns, and a county.

From 1834 to 1862, Sibley lived at St. Peters. There, as the American Fur Company's agent and the sutler at the fort, he came to know the people of the area: Dakota and Ojibwe Indians, French-Canadian and American fur traders, military men and their families, and early immigrants to the region. He hosted explorers, scientists, and wealthy tourists visiting from downriver. An avid sportsman with a stable of fine horses and two huge hunting dogs, he took long hunting trips in the beautiful woods and prairies of the area.

This is the story of those early years, when Sibley came to know Minnesota and Minnesota came to know Sibley.

One of the earliest known portraits of Henry H. Sibley, an image from around 1848 when he was 38 years old, now hangs in the Sibley House. MINNESOTA HISTORICAL SOCIETY.

Henry Sibley's Early Years

Henry H. Sibley, just over six feet tall, erect and muscular, with deep-set brown eyes and rugged features, was twenty-three years old and ready for new adventures when he came to St. Peters, now Mendota, Minnesota, in 1834. During most of the next twenty-eight years he would live in a fine stone house with a stable of horses and a collection of hunting dogs; enjoy the freedom to ride and hunt on the open prairies; play unofficial host to many visitors who came from the world down the Mississippi; and watch the cities of Minneapolis and St. Paul take hold and start to grow. As a fur trader he would number among his friends French-Canadians and mixed-bloods working for his company, the Dakota Indians with whom they did business on their western lands, and, across the river from his Mendota home, the officers at Fort Snelling, an international community of civilians who had settled in the shadow of the fort, and missionaries who had come to serve all. These were Sibley's friends and neighbors in his early days at Mendota when he was young and free and the open prairies and plains beckoned.[1]

Born in 1811 in Detroit, Sibley was the son of Solomon Sibley, a lawyer who had served his community as a legislator, congressman, and chief justice of Michigan Territory. Both his father and his mother, Sarah Sproat Sibley, were descended from colonial patriots and Revolutionary War officers; his elder brother attended the U.S. Military Academy at West Point and became a career officer in the U.S. Army. Sibley, who was not interested in a military career, was educated at an academy in Detroit, tutored for two years in Latin and Greek, and then entered his father's office for the study of law. He soon discovered that he did not want to be a lawyer and persuaded his parents to let him give up his legal studies. He loved the outdoors and had become a "master of the rifle, the fishing rod, and the canoe," according to historian William W. Folwell. Some kind of work that would give him time for outdoor activities appealed to him. With his parents' approval, in the summer of 1828, he took a position as clerk to the sutler (or storekeeper) at Fort Brady, a frontier military post near Sault Ste. Marie, Michigan. He was seventeen when he left Detroit.[2]

After only a few months Sibley quit the sutler's store and went to work for the widow of a fur trader, but in the spring of 1829 he left that position to take a clerkship in the Mackinac (pronounced Mackinaw) office of the American Fur Company. Mackinac was an important military post, strategically located between lakes Huron and Michigan. It was also the chief entrepôt for the American Fur Company's trade with the vast Great Lakes region and upper Mississippi valley. At Mackinac Sibley came to know officers of the Company as well as employee traders, clerks, and voyageurs.

The Company, organized by John Jacob Astor in 1808, had grown to control trade in furs across much of North America south of the Hudsons Bay Company territory in British America. The American Fur Company's agents and traders bartered with the Indians for furs—beaver, muskrat, buffalo, mink, marten, otter, and others—and supplied the blankets, guns, traps, ornaments, and other manufactured goods that the Indians wanted. The Company bought foreign goods for sale to the Indians and marketed its furs abroad in London, in Canton, and at yearly trade fairs in Leipzig. Beyond its trade in furs, the Company

In October 1838, Henry Sibley wrote a letter to his cousin Charles C. Trowbridge, from Sault Ste. Marie where he worked for the sutler at Fort Brady. In it he spoke of being "in a great hurry, as I have a great deal to do." SIBLEY HOUSE COLLECTION.

engaged in fisheries, steamboating, banking, farming, land speculation, and trade in agricultural products. Because of its economic and international activities it maintained a presence in Washington, D.C., attempting to influence governmental policies that could affect its business. Sibley worked for the Company for the next five years as clerk and purchasing agent.[3]

A man who knew him in those days remembered that once when Sibley was working behind the counter in the Company's Mackinac office, he encountered a "ruffianly fellow, a great bully, and a man of powerful physique, [who] had disputed Sibley's word. Quick as a flash young Sibley sprang over the counter, threw himself on the bully, and seizing him as one would a light bundle of goods, threw him out of the door. The fellow picked himself up and made off in haste." Another time, one of Sibley's employees, a "powerful and desperate fellow . . . while intoxicated" picked a quarrel with Sibley, who "saw no half-way measure would answer, or his authority would have been gone forever. He knocked the rascal down by a blow of his fist, and then pummeled him until he begged for mercy." It was reported that the man was seriously hurt. "Some days afterward Sibley sent him word to come back and behave himself, which he did and he [Sibley] never had any more trouble with the man nor indeed with any of the others [of his employees]."[4]

In 1832 Sibley took a new position. For most of two winters he traveled on horseback across Ohio and Pennsylvania as an agent purchasing flour, corn, pork, and tobacco, among other supplies, for the Company. By 1834, the future of the Company seemed uncertain in a changing market. Beaver, which had been the most popular and valuable of the furs it collected, was no longer in demand in the fashion world for hats; nutria from South America was beginning to compete in world markets with muskrat as a desirable fur. That summer John Jacob Astor sold the American Fur Company to a New York organization headed by Ramsay Crooks that kept the company name and many of its employees.

Only one year remained of Sibley's employment contract with the Company and he began thinking of other opportunities. His parents were opposed to his staying in "what was little better than a wild Indian country," he later wrote, and he had been offered positions in two banks, one in Michigan, the other in Ohio. He considered paying the Company $1,000 to release him from the obligation to stay in its employ another year. Instead, his love of the outdoors, the sporting life, its drama and excitement, and an opportunity to live in a "wonderful land of lake, prairie and forest" tempted him to remain with the Company.[5]

Ramsay Crooks, president of the new company and an old friend of Sibley's father, said that Sibley had served them well for five years and "was just the young man he [Crooks] wanted, to fill the important place of Agent of the Company." In that position Crooks promised that Sibley would have "exclusive control [of] a vast area of country, embracing many trading posts, and a small army of traders, clerks and voyageurs." Hercules Dousman, a fur trader from Prairie du Chien whom Sibley had come to know and consider a warm friend, urged Sibley to stay with the new company and take a position in one of its five regional districts. Sibley would be a partner with Dousman and Joseph Rolette, Sr., a veteran Prairie du Chien trader. Dousman would furnish the capital needed for the business and Sibley would manage the trade with the Dakota (or Sioux) Indians in a sub-district known as the Sioux Outfit in an area extending from above Lake Pepin north and west to the headwaters of rivers tributary to the Missouri.

Dousman told him of the charms of the region, describing plains "covered with buffalo and elk, while the woods abounded with bear, deer and other game animals, and the numerous lakes with aquatic fowl of every variety." Convinced by Crooks, Dousman, and his own inclinations, Sibley won his parents' approval of his new enterprise "which must necessarily add nearly a thousand miles to the distance which separated us." He was to be paid a salary of $1,200 a year and a share of the profits in the trade over a territory larger than France. Headquarters for

Alexis Bailly was the American Fur Company trader at St. Peters prior to Henry Sibley's arrival. Sibley boarded with him and his family during his first winter there. MINNESOTA HISTORICAL SOCIETY.

his Sioux Outfit was to be at St. Peters or Mendota, where the St. Peters (now Minnesota) River met the Mississippi.

In the summer employees of the Company brought to St. Peters furs gathered by the Indians during their winter and spring hunts in this vast western area. In the company warehouse at St. Peters, the furs were packed and prepared for transshipment by way of the Mississippi, Wisconsin, and Fox rivers and the Great Lakes for New York and world markets. There, too, the agent settled his accounts with his employees, contracted with them for the coming year, and provided them with the supplies and goods they needed for the next year's trade with the Indians. All of the land in this domain belonged to the Indians except for a small reserve at Fort Snelling, a frontier military post situated on a high bluff overlooking the two rivers.

From Mackinac to St. Peters

Sibley began the journey to his new home in the fall of 1834, taking a schooner from Mackinac to Green Bay on Lake Michigan.[6] From there he traveled on the Fox River to its portage with the Wisconsin River (at present-day Portage, Wisconsin). Then he boarded a small stern wheel steamer for a journey of five days in low water past numerous sandbars to Prairie du Chien on the Mississippi River. There he stayed several days with his partner, Dousman, preparing for a land journey of some three hundred miles to his new home at St. Peters, soon to be better known by its Indian name of Mendota.

At Prairie du Chien Sibley joined forces with Alexis Bailly, a trader who lived at St. Peters and was in charge of four stations or posts in Sibley's new district. The two men traveled together on horseback for the rest of the journey, taking with them a Winnebago Indian guide, two voyageurs, and sixteen-year-old Duncan Campbell, son of a fur trader and an Indian woman. Ice had begun to form on the Mississippi when they left Prairie du Chien. After a near catastrophe in crossing the river and the loss of their guide, who deserted after taking them at least two days to the west of their proper route, they finally found their way in the midst of a storm to the residence of Indian trader Augustin Rocque, near present-day Wabasha. Rocque's was the only white person's house they encountered on the overland journey to St. Peters. The Rocque family welcomed them, fed them well on a satisfying meal that included fresh venison and wild honey, and provided them with comfortable beds for the night. To add to their enjoyment, Sibley recalled, "Mr. Rocque had a pretty six-

Pilot Knob as watercolorist Seth Eastman viewed it from below Fort Snelling around 1847. A corner of Pike Island is visible at left. The American Fur Company trading post was outside the frame of the picture to the left. MINNESOTA HISTORICAL SOCIETY.

teen year old daughter, who vied with her parents, in endeavors to make our unexpected visit agreeable." Rested and in good cheer, they accomplished the rest of their journey without difficulty.

Sibley first saw the little settlement at St. Peters on October 28, 1834. Although he forgot the date and later mistakenly gave it as November 7, he never forgot the view. He wrote: "When I reached the brink of the hill [called Pilot Knob] overlooking the surrounding country I was struck with the picturesque beauty of the scene. From that outlook the course of the Mississippi River from the north, suddenly turning eastward to where St. Paul now stands, the Minnesota River from the west, the principal tributary of the main stream, and at the junction, rose the military post of Fort Snelling perched upon a high and commanding point, with its stone walls, and blockhouses, bidding defiance to any attempt at capture by the poorly armed savages, should such be made. There was also visible a wide expanse of prairie in the rear of the Fort."

Descending the hill, he was disappointed to see at close hand a cluster of dilapidated log buildings. Larger and more pretentious among them was the home of Bailly and his family, where Sibley would first live. Nearby were the homes of Bailly's father-in-law, fur trader Jean Baptiste Faribault; those of a blacksmith, carpenter, and voyageurs who worked for the Company; and the storehouse for the Company's goods and furs.[7]

Sibley was not impressed by the settlement and immediately decided that some of its buildings should be demolished. Reporting his arrival to Ramsay Crooks on November 1, Sibley recommended the construction of a smaller but more substantial building for his own residence and a new storehouse for the Company's goods and furs. He believed, and Bailly agreed, that it would be cheaper in the long run to construct new buildings than to keep the old log ones in repair.

Sibley lived with the Bailly family during his first winter at St. Peters. The Baillys were hospitable but the food, largely bread and pork, was monotonous. Heavy snow kept him from traveling very far out in the field to become acquainted with the territory, the traders, and the Indians with whom he would be doing business. With few duties and no domestic responsibilities in the Bailly household, Sibley had time to read and visit his neighbors. Any planned building awaited the coming of summer.

Henry Sibley's warehouse, the first building he built at St. Peters, is shown in a detail of an 1844 J. C. Wild painting. Fort Snelling is top right, and Pike Island below it.
MINNESOTA HISTORICAL SOCIETY.

Sibley's Bachelor Household

Alexis Bailly sold Sibley his fur trade property and his home at St. Peters in 1835 and moved with his family to near present-day Wabasha. Sibley stayed on in the Bailly log house for a number of years before his stone house was built. By the summer of 1835 he had hired a man who "could cook plain food moderately well, but who proved himself to be not only wasteful but withal not entirely cleanly in his methods for which faults I was compelled to reprimand him frequently and severely."

On August 1, he wrote to his mother that he had been at Prairie du Chien on Company business for three weeks and "with making out the Outfits of the traders & clerks in my Department, not to speak of my household Cares, I have had but little time even to sleep or eat. I have been in addition quite unwell but thanks to that kind Providence who has hitherto preserved me from danger, seen and unseen, I am now quite restored to health and am going on with my accustomed labors. . . . I have to see to my own cookery, in fact I make my own coffee, and scarcely a day passes that the Agent of the Grand Co. is not seen with sleeves rolled up, & towel in hand, washing castors or dishes, while his head is busy in devising means to get something to eat."

He had again hired domestic help and again was not satisfied. The wife and children were dirty; the children disturbed him with their crying. He began to think of looking for a wife. "I cannot live the life I now lead without somebody to help me." To his sister Mary he wrote yearningly of his mother's cooking—of her "mangoes [green muskmelon pickles], or pies or pound cake"—and said, "I milk my own cows, make my own pickles, wash my own dishes & make my own butter."[8]

While he struggled to organize his household, he began the construction of a "spacious stone warehouse which was completed the following year [1836–37], and [it] added greatly [not only] to the facilities for transacting business . . . but to the accomodations for lodging my numerous guests." To build the warehouse he hired a stonemason, John Miller or Mueller, who may have been a Swiss refugee from the Red River settlement, and a carpenter, Charles Mousseau.[9]

Lieutenant E. K. Smith's map of the Fort Snelling area in October 1837 showed a variety of new buildings around Henry H. Sibley's trading post. Sibley's house is the bulding to the right of the building at bottom left labeled "Ferribault's," the home of Jean Baptiste Faribault which still stands today. The other building at the top right with the same label is Alexander Faribault's cabin. MINNESOTA HISTORICAL SOCIETY.

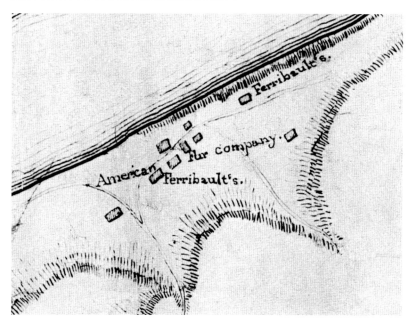

Sibley's house as it may have looked after its construction around 1837. Not shown are later additions such as a portico in front. LISA KRAHN DRAWING.

After the warehouse was completed work began on his stone residence. He hired Miller, Mousseau, and Amable Morant or Morin (also known as Amos Morand), a French-Canadian who was also a stonemason. His construction crew may have included fur trade employees, Dakota men and women, and off-duty soldiers.[10]

The stone residence, built away from the river and behind the warehouse, was described by his biographer Nathaniel West in the 1880s as "a building of plain but substantial character, . . . with a portico in front, entered not only from front and rear, but also by a flight of steps ascending outside to a small square gallery connecting with the second story, the whole inclosed in a garden surrounded by a picket fence."[11]

The structure was limestone from a nearby quarry. "The

laths were willows and rushes cut from the banks of the river, woven together with reeds and grasses. The insulation was mud and clay from the river banks mixed with straw. The larger timbers which were used for braces, joists, beams, floors, and window sills, were all hand hewn and joined together by wooden pegs. The roof was covered with clapboards and split by hand."[12]

In the original building were six rooms, a basement, and a garret or attic. Later additions included a four-room south section built in the 1840s and an office and porch added about 1850. In the basement kitchen was a large fireplace, where in the early days the cooking was done, and adjacent to it were two small cold-storage rooms.

A cutaway detail of the interior walls of Sibley's house reveals the infill that was made from materials on the banks of the river: willow saplings woven together, daubed with mud and straw. This is known as "wattle and daub." BRUCE WHITE PHOTO.

This decorative wrought-iron stove in the Sibley House was brought from Quebec in the 1830s. Stoves like this were shipped in pieces and assembled by local blacksmiths. BRUCE WHITE PHOTO.

Some three hundred feet from the house Sibley had a barn built where he kept horses and cattle, and nearby was a "capacious dog house divided into compartments to keep the pugnacious by themselves." Sibley's home and warehouse, the barn and other outbuildings, the Jean Baptiste Faribault House (1839-40) and the Hypolite Dupuis House (1854) all became part of the St. Peters fur trade settlement and are depicted in drawings and paintings of the later years of Sibley's residence there. Those buildings that have been preserved are now a part of the Sibley Historic Site.

Sibley lived at St. Peters as a bachelor until his marriage in 1843. His household later came to include his wife, his children, and members of his wife's family.

The Dakota and the Fur Trade

During his years as a fur trader at St. Peters, perhaps no other neighbors were more important to Sibley's well being than the Dakota Indians who gathered the furs and the traders who collected them for the Company.[13] Three bands of the Mdewakanton Sioux or Dakota (People of the Lakes) lived in summer villages on the western bank of the Mississippi—on the Wabasha prairie (near present-day Winona), at present-day Red Wing, and at Kaposia or Red Rock (present-day Newport). Three other bands lived in villages on the St. Peters River below present-day Shakopee. A seventh band lived on the shores of Lake Calhoun. Farther away in Sibley's trading area were bands of the Wahpekute, or People of the Shot Leaf, in the Cannon River region and near present-day Faribault. The lower Wahpetons, or People of the Leaf, lived near present-day Little Rapids, and in the vicinity of Belle Plaine; the upper Wahpeton were on the shores of Lac qui Parle; the upper and lower Sissetons occupied territory extending to Traverse des Sioux, Big Stone Lake, and Lake Traverse, and as far as the Coteau des Prairies. Still farther out on the Dakota prairies were other related western bands. Although the American Fur Company also traded with the Ojibwe in northern Minnesota and Wisconsin and bands of them often visited Fort Snelling, the Ojibwe were frequently in a state of warfare with the Dakota and were not a part of Sibley's Sioux Outfit. He met many of the men who worked for him during his first year at St. Peters, but not until the fall of 1835 was he able to take a tour of inspection of the posts in his domain.

At that time his principal posts were managed by

Black Dog's Village, southwest of St. Peters on the Minnesota River, from an engraving based on a drawing or painting by Adolf Hoeffler done in 1853. MINNESOTA HISTORICAL SOCIETY.

Joseph R. Brown, who had come to the region originally as a soldier, and other traders of French-Canadian origin: Louis Provençalle, Jean Baptiste Faribault, Joseph Laframboise, and Joseph Renville. The men who worked for the traders were French-Canadian voyageurs, regularly hired for three-year terms. Sibley came to know those who worked for his Sioux Outfit as hardworking and trustworthy men. They often lived on daily rations of two ounces of beef or buffalo tallow and a quart of hulled corn supplemented with wild game they were able to shoot.

In later years, Sibley remembered them fondly: "The labors of these voyageurs, especially during the winter season, were excessively severe as they were compelled to carry packages of fifty or one hundred pounds weight, frequently for days together, in visiting distant Indian camps, and to return laden with buffalo robes and the skins of other animals. Sometimes it occurred that they were overtaken by the snow and were fain to take shelter under a drift, there to remain until the storm subsided. And yet under all such circumstances of toil and exposure, these men were ordinarily cheerful and unmurmuring, and withal faithful to their trust."[14] They became longtime residents of the territory and took wives from among the Dakota tribes with whom they traded. They and their families were prominent early-day Minnesota pioneers.

Sibley soon became acquainted with many of the Dakota bands and began to learn their language. They named him Wah-ze-o-man-zee, or Walker-in-the-Pines; he visited their villages, went hunting with them, and entertained them at his headquarters. After he came to know them well he called them the "Most warlike and passionate of all the Indian tribes upon the continent . . . yet [they were] not without many noble traits of character." They were in some ways "in advance of the white man's boasted Christian culture, especially in the observance of the rules and laws of natural morality." They were honest—it was considered disgraceful for a warrior to steal; they valued female chastity; they cared for their widows and orphans; they believed in a Gitchi Manitou, or Good Spirit, and in many minor spirits, who, if given sacrifices of tobacco and other articles, would protect them from disease, disaster, and death, but they seemed to have no concept of a life beyond death. Sibley's view of the Dakota, as expressed in his own writings and quoted by Nathaniel West, referred to the Indians at a time before whites acquired their lands and Euro-American domination left them "stranded wreck[s] in the great ocean of existence."[15]

Sometime during his early years at St. Peters Sibley formed a relationship with Red Blanket Woman, of Black Dog's Village.[16] She was the daughter of Bad Hail (or Wicked Hail) a Mdewakanton chief (or sub-chief), and she may have had a French-Canadian ancestor. Sibley and Red Blanket Woman became the parents of a daughter in 1841. In that year Sibley's assistant, William H. Forbes, sponsored the daughter's baptism by Catholic missionary Father Augustin Ravoux as Helen or Helene (she was more often known as Helen Hastings Sibley). Her Indian name was Wa-ki-ye, The Bird; but she was also known as Muzza-wakan-win. Her mother is said to have married another man and died about 1843.

Sibley made provision for Helen's care and education in the home of William R. Brown, a teacher and farmer of the Methodist mission at Red Rock, and his wife Martha. Helen was living with the Browns in St. Paul in the 1850s and in 1859, in their home, married Sylvester Sawyer, a young doctor who had boarded with the Browns. Sibley, her father, gave her away. After their marriage, the couple moved to Milwaukee. A year later, Helen died of scarlet fever after giving birth to a daughter, who died a week later.

Years after Helen's death (and the death of the woman he later married), Sibley wrote in his autobiography of an encounter with a young Indian woman during his first years at Mendota, suggesting how such a relationship as his could have occurred.[17] "It was the custom in those days, to leave the doors of all buildings unlocked, save only those of the stores where goods and provisions were kept, and I was lying in bed in the log house, shortly after my return from the long trip, engaged in reading, when about midnight, a male, and female Indian, entered very much to my surprise. I mastered enough of the Sioux tongue to understand the purport of common conversation, and I asked the man what had brought him to my room at that untimely hour? He took his companion by the hand, and led her to my bedside, and I recognized in her the young, and good looking daughter of the Indian before me, who was a sub-chief of one of the lower bands. He commenced by saying, that he was about to depart to make his winter hunt, many days march away, and would not return until late in the spring, and as he did not wish to expose his young daughter to hardship & suffering, he had decided to ask me to take her in charge. The poor girl meantime, stood there awaiting my reply, having covered her head with the blanket she wore. I excused myself to the father, telling him it would be wrong in me to comply with his offer, that I had no intention of taking to myself an Indian maiden for a wife, for many reasons I could not explain to him, except one which he could comprehend, and that was, it would make the other Indians, and their families, dissatisfied and jealous." Accepting Sibley's reply the two left, "both of them disappointed, and mortified, at the ill success of their mission."

In attempting to explain matters further, Sibley continued, "It must not be supposed, that from an Indian point of view, there was anything savoring of immodesty in the proceedings I have narrated. It was considered a laudable ambition on the part of a Sioux girl, to capture a respectable white man, and become his wife without any legal ceremony, but the connection was regarded as equally obligatory on both parties, and in many cases ended only

Seth Eastman painted this watercolor in the 1840s or 1850s of Medicine Bottle's Village, located on the Mississippi below present-day St. Paul. MINNESOTA HISTORICAL SOCIETY.

with the death of one of them. I shall have more to write on this subject farther on, when I will demonstrate, that female virtue was held in as high estimation among the Sioux bands in their wild state, as by the whites, and the line between the chaste, and the *demi-monde*, quite as well defined."

Sibley may have intended to write more about his own relationship, but his story ends abruptly at this point. Other than traces of payments made for his daughter's care, he left little more information about Helen or her mother. When Lieutenant James McClure, an officer friend who married an Indian woman, was killed in the Florida wars, Sibley also took some responsibility for their daughter, Nancy McClure, who later married fur trader David Faribault.

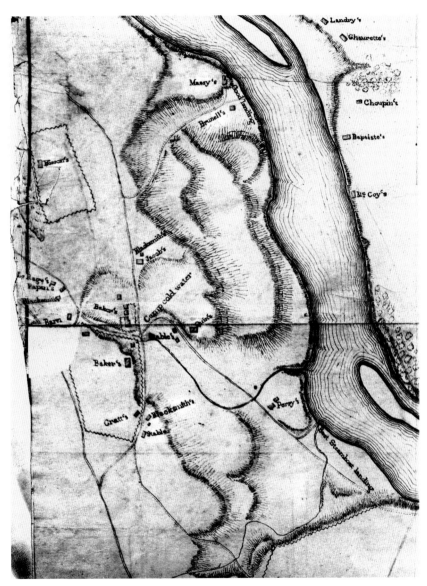

A portion of Lieutenant E. K. Smith's October 1837 map of the Fort Snelling Reservation shows the area adjacent to Coldwater Spring northeast of the fort where Benjamin F. Baker's trading post and a number of homes of early settlers were located. Sibley dealt with these people as customers and as suppliers of wood, charcoal, cattle, and other supplies.
MINNESOTA HISTORICAL SOCIETY.

The Community at Fort Snelling

Close at hand and on the bluff were Sibley's military neighbors. Scattered about on both sides of the river bank and spread out on the prairie beyond Fort Snelling lived an interesting multi-racial assortment of people.[18] Among them were families of Scottish and Irish descent and Swiss emigrants from the Selkirk Colony on the Red River of the North; a few retired soldiers; some blacks or mixed-race blacks (mainly servants of officers); Dakota Indians; and French-Canadian fur traders, some of whom worked for Sibley and others for independent trader Benjamin F. Baker, who was building a new stone house adjacent to Coldwater (or Cold Water) Spring. In a cluster of buildings on the prairie about a quarter of a mile west of the fort were the log and stone headquarters of the government Indian Agent Lawrence Taliaferro, who issued the licenses that permitted Sibley and his employees to conduct their trade. Living farther out on the prairie near an Indian village on Lake Calhoun were the first of the Protestant missionaries to begin activities among the Dakota. All of these neighbors Sibley would meet in due course, but he found his first congenial friends among the military.

Sibley presented himself at the fort very soon after his arrival at St. Peters, bringing letters of introduction to officers of the First Infantry stationed there. Welcomed into the community, Sibley spent many hours in their company during the winter. John Bliss, Jr., son of the post commandant, remembered meeting Sibley, "a very young man, but uncommonly large, strong and fine looking, with a very pleasant, and frank, but determined face. He was in the employ of some fur company, and the very man for that hard, wild, venturesome life." Young Bliss recalled much sociability among the officers, as they played cards, dominos, checkers, and chess. Sibley, he said "was a good chess player, and for that time was a wonder of correct and temperate habits, and by my father and the officers generally was held in high esteem." Sibley said that "the game of chess was the favorite amusement in [the] garrison, officers and ladies participating."[19]

Among Sibley's special military friends were Lieutenant James McClure, the local quartermaster officer; Major Gustavus Loomis, second in command at the fort, and his family; and Lieutenant Edmund A. (Ned) Ogden of Company D, who married the daughter of Major Loomis. During the winter, Ogden, with other officers and perhaps with Sibley, spent evenings in the company of interpreter Scott Campbell (brother of Duncan, who had accompanied Sibley's party from Prairie du Chien). Curious about the language of the Dakota, they compiled a dictionary of useful words, surely helpful to Sibley in his own dealings with the Indians. Ogden later gave their compilation to the missionaries Samuel and Gideon Pond and, wrote the Ponds, "these words and definitions with what we had gathered from other sources, made quite an encouraging beginning of the Dakota and English Lexicon which was long after edited by the Rev. Stephen R. Riggs and published by the Smithsonian Institution."[20]

Holiday entertainments at the fort could well have included Sibley. On Christmas Eve Major Bliss and his wife entertained at a splendid supper "consisting among other delicacies of the season of venison, roast pig, sausage, mince & pumpkin pies, new year's cake, and many other kickshaws too numerous to mention." On Christmas morning at ten the Loomis family entertained at a

A view from the Fort Snelling Round Tower looking east across the interior of the fort toward Mendota. The German artist Adolf Hoeffler did the original painting or drawing on which this 1853 engraving was based.
MINNESOTA HISTORICAL SOCIETY.

dejeuner à la fourchette (brunch). For several hours in the afternoon, parties from the fort took sleigh rides up the Mississippi River to the Falls of St. Anthony. There, at the site of government saw and grist mills, a cattle corral, and quarters for extra duty men who worked there, they could stop for a hot drink. On this Christmas Day they returned for a "superb" supper in the acting sutler's quarters. Music and singing ended the day's festivities.[21]

In the jollifications that continued during the week between Christmas and the New Year, sleigh riding was the principal outdoor recreation of the fort community. On December 29 three men and a dog train arrived from the Red River country with Hudson's Bay Company mail to be forwarded to England by way of Prairie du Chien.

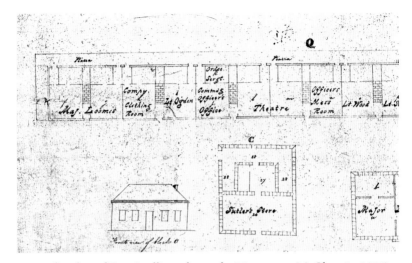

Part of a plan of Fort Snelling, drawn by Lieutenant McClure in 1835, shows the quarters of Major Loomis and Lieutenants Ogden and Wood, the company clothing room, the commanding officer's office, the theatre, and the sutler's store. NATIONAL ARCHIVES.

The surgeon Dr. Nathan Jarvis said the body of the sleigh was made of deerskin in the shape of a shoe and "large enough to stretch yourself at length." It was drawn by four dogs harnessed in line, the leading dog wearing a string of small silver bells around his neck. On the journey from Red River the dogs ran fifty miles a day carrying two of the men and a considerable amount of baggage. The men took turns riding and running alongside, with the runner sometimes going ahead on snowshoes, breaking trail.

On the night of December 30, the Thespians, an amateur group of enlisted men and non-commissioned officers, performed two plays, "The Honest Thieves" and "The Wag of Windsor," interspersed with comic songs. Sibley, who had been a member of an amateur theatrical group in Detroit, was soon able to encourage the Fort Snelling Thespians' activities when he became a sutler.[22]

Sibley Becomes a Storekeeper

Sibley had clerked only a few months in the sutler store at Fort Brady, but in his new position at St. Peters he had become convinced that it would be useful for him as a fur trader to also become identified with the sutling business. Learning that a new military post was to be established on the Des Moines River, he tried unsuccessfully to obtain the appointment as its sutler as a prudent move in safeguarding the Company's fur trade business from possible competitors. Although the sutler's main duty was to supply the troops with goods that were not provided by government issue, he could also sell goods to civilians and Indians. If the fur trader could also be sutler "in the vicinity of a garrison . . . in a hundred ways it can be made to appear to the simple Indians that their 'Great Father' would be pleased to have them give their furs to one who is so nearly connected with his soldiers."[23]

The sutler could operate his business rent free within the stockade and he could make use of a familiar network of wholesale houses and financial connections in purchasing the great variety of goods needed for the store. On the other hand, offsetting these advantages was the probability that he would not make much money. The sutler's business operations were controlled by officers of the garrison in a military Council of Administration, which set prices for goods, took a percentage of the profits, and required the sutler to perform other services to the military. On balance, despite the drawbacks, the Company and its agent concluded that if they controlled the sutler business, they could reduce the potential influence of possible competitors in the fur trade.

When Samuel C. Stambaugh, the former editor of a country newspaper in Pennsylvania, a man of political influence, and the newly appointed sutler at Fort Snelling, arrived at his post in the fall of 1835, he came as one without experience in the business who had made no arrangements for stocking the store for the coming year. After a time of dickering and negotiating, Sibley and Dousman agreed to manage the business and pay Stambaugh half the profits. When Stambaugh and Sibley became partners, Ramsay Crooks in New York forwarded to the post goods for the 1836 season. In the end it was Sibley, with the financial backing of the Company, who ran the business. The inventories, cash books, and ledgers that detail his dealings with officers, enlisted men, civilians, fur traders, and Indians provide glimpses of everyday life at the fort and in Sibley's neighborhood during the next three years.

The sutler sold a wide variety of goods, as did a typical frontier general store of the period. On his shelves were yard goods, clothing, hardware, household furnishings, kitchenwares, food, beer, and wines. He handled the laundry for the men of the regiment, engaging women (wives of enlisted men or civilians in the neighborhood) to do the work. He sold fresh-baked bread from the army bake house and remitted a portion of its sale to the army commissary. He collected fees for the post library. When the soldiers had a celebration, he sold them what they needed in food and drinks and collected from each member of the entertainment committee his share of the bill. When a soldier died, a committee of his mates purchased black ribbon and other necessities for his funeral, and each member of the committee paid the sutler his share of the expense.

From civilians who lived in the area, the sutler took in

Sibley's sutler accounts record dealings with Jacob Falstrom, an early Swedish settler and former fur trader who lived in the Coldwater area. In addition to supplying the sutler with firewood, Falstrom purchased a variety of supplies. MINNESOTA HISTORICAL SOCIETY.

trade such goods as eggs, maple syrup, firewood, and deer and calf skins, and in turn he sold these products to anyone who wanted them. For the amusement of the civilian and military community, he sold fiddles, fiddle strings, skins and sticks for drums, games, cards, and books. He maintained a standing account with the men of the Thespian Society, supplying them with fabrics, paint, pasteboard, and a variety of other necessities for mounting their plays. He sold tickets for their productions.[24]

His customers usually and eventually paid their bills. Regularly, military men ran up accounts that were not paid until the military paymaster visited the fort. Sometimes when the paymaster was delayed, he arranged for

The Benjamin F. Baker House, at top, and other buildings below it, adjacent to Coldwater Spring are shown above in a detail from an 1845 Henry Lewis painting. MINNESOTA HISTORICAL SOCIETY. *Baker's stone house was built around the same time as Sibley's. Below, Lawrence Taliaferro, in 1853, drew the Baker House when it was operated as the McKenzie Hotel.* NATIONAL ARCHIVES.

the Company to advance funds to pay the troops, for which it would be later reimbursed. At times when men were ordered to a new post before they were able to settle their accounts, the sutler forwarded and collected their bills from the sutler at their new post. In this and other ways, Sibley operated, with the backing of the Company, as a branch bank headquartered in the sutler store.

All of these services and more, Sibley and his clerks in the sutler store provided for the military and civilian community. More than that, when the Company was awarded a contract to handle the mail, the post office in the sutler store kept a record of letters received and sent by destinations and postage paid, listed the publications that came to the post office, and paid the man who carried the mail to and from Prairie du Chien.

After a year of handling the sutlership with its many duties and limited profit, taking inventory, ordering goods for the coming year, and dealing with an increasingly troublesome partner, Sibley wanted to get out of the business. When neither he nor representatives of the Company in the East were able to come to a reasonable agreement with Stambaugh, Sibley remained in the business for the duration of his contract. Even when Benjamin F. Baker, a rival fur trader, succeeded Stambaugh, Sibley was not free of the business. After Baker died in St. Louis in 1839, leaving his financial affairs in confusion, Sibley was called back to help the administrator settle Baker's accounts. Yet despite the many frustrations of the business, Sibley in the sutler store gained a wide and intimate knowledge of his military and civilian neighbors during his early years at St. Peters.[25]

The Indian Agency

In carrying on his fur trade business Sibley frequently called on the Indian Agent, Major Lawrence Taliaferro.[26] In August 1835, for example, he presented bonds and obtained licenses for two of his men, Joseph Laframboise and Alexander Faribault, to engage in the fur trade for the coming year. The Agent greeted Sibley cordially, but it was well known to both that relations between the agent and Sibley's predecessor, Alexis Bailly, had not been friendly. Frequent disputes between the two over real and sometimes fancied infractions of rules had given the American Fur Company a bad reputation in Taliaferro's mind. While disputes continued, Taliaferro, who had known and respected members of Sibley's family, found the new Company representative more agreeable.

But meeting the Agent on August 28, Sibley was indignant. Taliaferro noted, "Mr. Sibley stated that he understood that it had been reported to me that Beer had been given at his house to Indians. He had given his word of honor that no liquor should be given not even Porter or Beer and this I recollected. He had not given any nor would any be given at the same [and Sibley] authorised me to say for him that the accusation was groundless and false and that he was responsible for the remark."

Taliaferro accepted Sibley's explanation with "every confidence," and at year's end complimented the trader "for his cheerful cooperation with me in all that relates to Indian intercourse . . . and from my knowledge of your character and views I feel assured that you will unite with me in forwarding any course of policy to attain to our object not only with the Government but with everyone interested in the tranquility of the country."

Indian Agent Lawrence Taliaferro as shown in a portrait possibly painted by George Catlin around 1830. Visible at left is the council house along the Minnesota River bluffs where Taliaferro met with many Indian leaders, and an Indian encampment.
MINNESOTA HISTORICAL SOCIETY.

Detail showing the Council House.

Detail showing an Indian encampment below Fort Snelling.

The Religious Community

Sibley's family had been Episcopalians and for two years in Detroit he had been tutored by an Episcopalian clergyman (later missionary and army chaplain) the Rev. Richard F. Cadle. At Mackinac he joined the Presbyterian church and taught a Sunday School class. Generally, even when traveling or hunting, he tried to observe the Sabbath. A missionary friend, hearing that Sibley would be living at St. Peters, wrote: "The Lord in his providence has thrown you into a modern Sodom," and advised him that while "diligent in business" he should be "fervent in spirit serving the Lord."[27]

Shortly after his introduction to the officers at Fort Snelling, and among them members of its small religious contingent, Sibley and an officer (probably either Lieutenant Ogden or Major Loomis) set out on horseback one November day, traveling some eight miles to visit Samuel and Gideon Pond, who like Sibley had arrived in the area within the year. The two brothers from Connecticut, living in a log house on the east side of Lake Calhoun, had experienced a religious conversion some years before and decided to come to the Indian country as independent missionaries. While they were not trained for the mission field and were not sponsored by any church organization, according to historian Theodore C. Blegen, "they were not without qualifications for the work they proposed to do. They had enjoyed an excellent elementary schooling, had worked on farms, knew how to use their hands, and had practical good sense, simplicity of taste and habit, active and inquiring minds, persistence, and quiet courage." Both men, Blegen said, "were over six feet tall, stalwart and

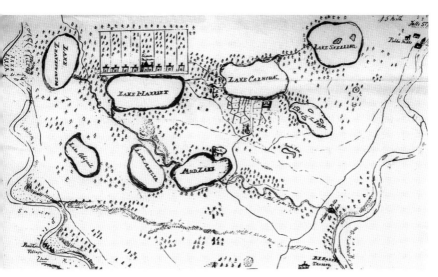

Indian Agent Lawrence Taliaferro drew this impressionistic map of the present-day Minneapolis area in the 1830s, with North at the right side. The mission school at Lake Harriet is shown at the top and the Dakota village at Lake Calhoun to its right. From top left flows the "St. Peters" (Minnesota) River, and Taliaferro has shown several Dakota villages next to it. The three lakes at bottom appear to correspond to present-day Mother, Nokomis, and Hiawatha. Minnehaha Falls is located at lower right. MINNESOTA HISTORICAL SOCIETY.

A detail from Taliaferro's map shows the mission school built by Jedediah Stevens and Samuel and Gideon Pond on the west shore of Lake Harriet. MINNESOTA HISTORICAL SOCIETY.

sinewy, alert and genial." They saw as their first major task learning the Dakota language so that they could present their religious message in the Indians' own tongue.[28]

Officers at the fort and the Indian Agent encouraged them in their mission. Cloud Man, or Man of the Sky, a friendly chief of the Mdewakanton Dakota, had chosen the site for their house near his village at a place on a hill where, Samuel later wrote, "the loons would be visible on the lake."[29]

Samuel Pond told a Connecticut correspondent how to find the place by the route Sibley and his friend would have taken.[30] "Leaving Fort Snelling and traveling northwest you would cross a green and level prairie three miles wide when you would come to a beautiful stream of water. . . . It is called by the Indians 'the little river' [present-day Minnehaha Creek]. There are a few trees each side of it. It issues out of a lake a short distance above the place where we cross it, and a little ways below it falls I think nearly a hundred feet [Minnehaha Falls]. This is a beautiful cataract & I seldom pass by it without going to see it."

Beyond the crossing of the little stream the trail extended through trees lining its bank north and north west over a hill and up following an Indian trail to the top of another hill, where white cloths fastened to poles marked Indian graves at a burial ground. Beyond the cemetery a turn to the right would take the riders through a cornfield by way of "A narrow lane which the women have fenced by setting up posts about as large as a persons wrist & tying slender poles to them with bark leads through the cornfields to the village." In the village were several small houses and fourteen larger ones where two or three families lived. Major Taliaferro named the village Eatonville in honor of Secretary of War John H. Eaton.

Beyond the village, "turning to the right along the east bank of the lake & ascending a hill through the woods," the riders would come to the log house of the Ponds, set within a four-acre tract the brothers had cleared and enclosed with a log fence. They had built the house that summer of oak logs cut on the property; they roofed the building with bark; they gathered stones on the lake shore for their fireplace.[31]

Agent Taliaferro found them temporary storage space in one of the agency buildings, loaned them tools, and gave them a window and a lock for their door. Major Bliss arranged for them to have some lumber and pine slabs from the army sawmill and gave them potatoes to eat and to plant the next season; Mrs. Bliss gave them a ham. Dakota people had brought them ducks, venison, potatoes, and corn, but the Ponds' usual fare before they could plant a garden of their own was fried pork with flour gravy.

They built their house the summer of 1834 to the sound of Indians screeching to scare redwing blackbirds from their cornfields and the torments of mosquitoes "active, vigorous, able-bodied. . . champion warriors every one of them," wrote Samuel.

As winter came on the Ponds settled in their house. They warmed themselves outdoors splitting wood; indoors they kept warm by their wood fire and by firelight committed scriptures to memory, devised a Dakota alphabet, and worked on a Dakota dictionary and grammar. There at Lake Calhoun, Sibley and his friend came to call.[32]

On November 14, Gideon wrote: "We have had a visit to-day from 2 men professors of religion[,] one an officer from Fort [Snelling] who has been there 2 or 3 months and the other a trader who has been here a month. We had a prayer meeting in our house[;] 4 of us were here. The

Dakota tipis as shown by Adolf Hoeffler in 1853. HARPER'S NEW
MONTHLY MAGAZINE.

Trader [Sibley] is a temperance man and expects to take
the plac[e] of one [Bailly] who smuggled and sold whiskey
to the Indians." The arrival of Sibley at St. Peters was "one
of the remarkable occurrences which has taken place while
we have been here for which we have great cause for grati-
tude." Had Bailly remained "in charge of that important
station, and centre of influence, we should have had no
friends on that side of the river."[33]

At the fort the Ponds, as did Sibley, counted both
Major Loomis and Lieutenant Ogden among their firm
friends. Loomis, the central figure in the fort's religious

community and second in rank to Major Bliss, was known among the soldiers as "Old Ring" because his preferred form of punishment for an erring soldier was a sentence to march around and around the parade ground carrying a heavy billet of wood on his back. As diligent in religion as he was in military matters, at a time when the fort had no chaplain, Loomis held Sunday services, weekday prayer meetings, and revival meeings that were said to have converted ten or twelve soldiers and a number of women attached to the garrison. The Ponds, who frequently attended the meetings, put the numbers of converts at fifteen or more and said that Loomis conducted prayer meetings as though he were commanding the troops. "'Nutt pray,' 'Ogden pray' was his usual method of directing his subordinates to take part in meeting."[34]

Meanwhile during the winter, the Ponds studied the Dakota language and when an epidemic of whooping cough ravaged Cloud Man's Village, they made coffins for the children who died.[35] In spring 1835 they helped their Dakota friends plant their crops, and in May they welcomed the missionary families of Dr. Thomas S. Williamson, Alexander Huggins, and the Rev. Jedediah Dwight Stevens. Rev. Stevens, with the help of the Ponds, built a home and boarding school for Indian children at Lake Harriet; the others moved on to Lac qui Parle. They were followed in the next few years by Samuel Francis Denton and Daniel Gavin, Protestant missionaries from Switzerland; Methodists led by the Rev. Alfred Brunson; and Catholic priests recruited in Europe by Bishop Mathias Loras. All became Sibley's friends.[36]

On June 11, 1835, in one of the company rooms at Fort Snelling, Sibley joined Major Loomis, his military associates, and members of the fur trade and mission community in organizing a Presbyterian church to be known as the Church of St. Peter, and later as the First Presbyterian Church of Minneapolis. Sibley, who brought a transfer of membership from the church at Mackinac, was elected one of the ruling elders, and for some years acted as clerk of the congregation.[37]

Although he continued his association with the Presbyterians, Sibley contributed to the building of the St. Peters Catholic church, which served many of his French-Canadian fur trade employees. In the 1840s he financed the building of a Protestant church, open to any denomination; the building later became a Mendota public school. A Catholic priest baptized his daughter Helen, but Sibley found her a home with a Methodist family. Later in the 1840s he renewed his association with the Episcopalians.[38]

Sibley described his own religious beliefs and practices in a letter to J. Fletcher Williams in 1877. He wrote: "I am a believer in the cardinal doctrines of the Christian faith,

After a narrow escape from death on a buffalo hunt in 1842, Sibley wrote:

I did not fail to render due homage to that Almighty Being who had so wonderfully preserved my life. The frequenter of Nature's vast solitudes may be a wild and reckless, but he cannot be esssentially an irreligious man. The solemn silence of forest and prairie—the unseen dangers which are incident to this mode of life, and the consciousness that Providence alone can avert them; all these have the effect to lead even the thoughtless man, occasionally, to reflection.[39]

having been educated in that belief, and never having swerved from it. I am an attendant regularly upon the Episcopal service and a vestryman in St. Paul parish in our city. I am not a communicant, for the reason that I am not a sectarian, and none of the denominations come up to my idea of what the church militant of Jesus Christ should be. Theology has loaded what I regard as a very clear and simple creed, with so much unnecessary mystification and ceremonial, that I shrink from the labor of penetrating the Labyrinth and prefer to turn to the pages of sacred writ for guidance. . . . I trust the time will come, sooner or later, when all Christians will cease controversies upon non-essential points, and unite in an unbroken front against infidelity in all its forms. I believe the doctrines of the Bible to be the only safe guide for nations, as well as individuals."[40]

"There being no hotel, or other accomodations for travellers," Sibley extended hospitality to an interesting assortment of visitors who ventured up the Mississippi by steamboat on what became known as "the fashionable tour" from Galena, St. Louis, and even from New Orleans. He wrote, "I was the host necessarily, of not only the many who bore letters of introduction to me, but of all of genteel appearance, whose wandering propensities led them to visit this distant region, so that I had to provide food, and lodging, such as they were, very frequently for fifteen or twenty men at a time. As no charge was ever made, some of these strangers would prolong their stay much longer than good manners, not to say decency, would dictate."[41]

Even before his warehouse–guest house was completed, Sibley's hospitality provided visiting dignitaries such other services as horses and guides. Best known of the summer visitors in 1835 was the artist George Catlin, who with his wife arrived on the steamboat *Warrior* in late June. At Fort Snelling Major Bliss provided a room in the officer quarters for Catlin's use; Agent Taliaferro arranged for him to meet both Dakota and Ojibwe Indians. Taliaferro said that the artist "has been engaged for years, & is still zealously progressing in the fine arts[;] he has secured the most valuable & authentic specimens of 30 Indian Tribes—their dresses, ceremonies, Buffalo Hunts dances &c &c with many paintings & views of Scenery which will go to shew the vast material for observation & cultivation in the remote territories[;] the great world know[s] nothing as yet of these things and it seems that it has been

Ah-no-je-hahge, or He who stands on both sides, a Dakota ballplayer pictured by George Catlin in 1835 at Fort Snelling. Catlin wrote that he painted the young man and others, "in the dress in which they had just struggled in the play."

left to Mr Catlin to open the sluices of information & by the magic of his pencil to hold the mirror up to public view."[42]

While at Fort Snelling Catlin painted portraits of both Dakota and Ojibwa Indians; he sketched the Ojibwe dancing and the Dakota playing ball. Then he looked to Sibley for help in planning a westward journey. Sibley wrote of him, "Being furnished with letters to military officers and civilians on the frontier, he was aided in every manner possible. His object in coming here was to visit the Pipe Stone quarry, and I furnished horses, without charge for himself and his companion, Mr [Robert S.] Wood English gentleman of intelligence, provided them with a trusty Indian guide, and gave them also letters to

While visiting Fort Snelling in 1835, George Catlin drew these cradleboards used by Dakota women, and showed how they were used on foot and on horseback.

the gentlemen at the head of my trading posts on the route, which rendered it quite certain that they would meet with no impediment from the Indians."[43]

Catlin's accounts of his experiences were highly misleading, according to Sibley. "His letters abounded with mis-statements, and the voluminous work subsequently produced by him was equal to them in that respect. The people in this quarter were absolutely astounded at his misrepresentations of men and things." In Sibley's view the "one redeeming feature in his book . . . is, his sketches of Indian faces and scenes, which are sufficiently faithful, as he was skillful in that line, and his pencil could not, therefore, like his pen, vary much from the truth."

Wa-nah-de-tunck-a, or Big Eagle, leader of the Black Dog Dakota village, was depicted by George Catlin in 1835.

Catlin's wife left Fort Snelling by steamboat in mid-July. After his visit to the Pipestone region, Catlin traveled down river by canoe. Shortly after his departure a party estimated to be some two hundred emigrants, traveling by oxcart from the Red River settlement, reached St. Peters driving horses and some fifty or sixty head of cattle. Among the many Scots in the party was one who appeared at the fort in "highland" costume, with plaid kilt and bonnet. Dr. Jarvis said the Indians who saw him were much delighted, thinking his costume similar to their own. Some of the emigrants may have joined others from the Red River who were living near the fort, but others moved down the Mississippi to new homes in Illinois or Indiana.[44]

St. Anthony Falls, pictured here by George Catlin, was a popular destination for visitors to the Minnesota region in the 1830s.

By early August, according to Dr. Jarvis, from one to two hundred other visitors had come to the fort. From season to season the numbers were constantly increasing, Jarvis observed, and he would not have been surprised to learn that in a few years the area would rival Niagara Falls in popularity. Talaiferro declared the climate to be unsurpassed during at least half a year "on the face of the habitable Globe as far as has been explored either for health or as an object of enterprise." He, too, had no doubt that because of climate, excellent water, sports, and hunting, "this country will become a place of great & fashionable resort for the man of pleasure, enterprise & spirit."[45]

The last visitor of note to come to St. Peters in 1835 was the Englishman and geologist George W. Featherstonhaugh, who arrived on September 12 on an expedition to the Blue Earth and other western headwaters of the St. Peters River. Featherstonaugh and his assistant, Lieutenant William W. Mather, came upriver to Fort Snelling in a thirty-five-foot birchbark canoe paddled by five French-Canadian voyageurs. In hiring his canoemen, Featherstonhaugh had required, among other qualifications, that they "should be well acquainted with the popular Canadian airs, and be able to sing them after the approved fashion of keeping time with their paddles." The good cheer generated by the voyageurs' tunes, unfortunately, did not permeate the discourse between Featherstonhaugh and his assistant. Well before their arrival at the fort, Featherstonhaugh had quarreled with Mather. Speaking to him seldom and rarely, he mentioned him not at all in the final report of his explorations.[46]

At St. Peters, Featherstonhaugh ordered his canoemen to make camp below the fort and he climbed the hill to pay his respects to Major Bliss. The commandant arranged to have the visitor's baggage sent to a vacant room and invited him to tea that evening. When no one asked him to dinner, Featherstonhaugh left the fort, found his way down the bluff to the river, and had his men ferry him across to Sibley's residence. There he presented other letters of introduction and a request for a good guide and interpreter to go with him on his geological explorations.[47]

"Mr. Sibley received me very kindly, and immediately offered me quarters at his house, which I certainly should have accepted, if I had not thought it would give umbrage at the fort," said Featherstonhaugh. As for a guide and interpreter, Sibley had "exactly the sort of person" Featherstonhaugh needed. The man was known as Milor, "a fine French-man-looking Indian, about fifty-five years old, tall and active, and was, as he told me, the son of a French officer by a Saukie [Sac?] woman." Milor was well acquainted with the country where Featherstonhaugh hoped to travel, and he could speak both French and

Dakota. The geologist was pleased with his appearance and conversation and considered himself fortunate in having such a person for his expedition.[48]

Featherstonhaugh seems to have found Sibley's company agreeable but he could not stay longer with him because of the "horrible atmosphere of tobacco smoke I had been obliged to breathe at the agency of the fur company, where all hands appeared to be constantly smoking." Seized by a violent and nervous sick headache, Featherstonhaugh excused himself and returned to the fort, expecting—hoping—to find there a comfortable room and bed.

It was not to be. At the hands of an orderly, he was taken to the place where his baggage had preceded him. "It was an old dirty, ill-smelling, comfortless store-room, which had been assigned to me to sleep in: it appeared never to have been swept out, and the floor was covered with casks and boxes, and all sorts of unseemly things. No bed, no mattress, nothing, not even a light had been provided for me."

From conversations with officers who later saw his lodgings and commiserated with him, Featherstonhaugh came to the conclusion that the person at fault in assigning his quarters was not Major Bliss but his second in command, Major Loomis, of whom he developed a most unflattering opinion. Yet not wishing to cause any disturbance between the "manly soldier-like" commandant and the "mundungus" Major Loomis, the visitor endured his bedroom in the "musty and melancholy store-room" until he left to travel up the St. Peters River.

On the morning of September 17, Featherstonaugh and his party set off in "a fine sweet fresh breeze, and [with] a world of adventure" before them. They were gone a month in their geological explorations as far as the Blue Earth

Mendota, as it appeared around 1845, is depicted in Seth Eastman's oil painting Mendota from Fort Snelling, *from the Zimmerman Family Collection. A detail, below, shows four large buildings, including, from left to right, a wooden warehouse, Sibley's stone warehouse, the Sibley house, and at far right, the Jean Baptiste Faribault house.*

Elizabeth Dillon Talia-
ferro, the wife of Indian
Agent Lawrence Talia-
ferro. During evenings at
Major Taliaferro's house,
the explorer Joseph Nicollet
played the violin accompa-
nied by Mrs. Taliaferro on
the piano, and at bedtime,
Mrs. Taliaferro fed Nicollet
a supper of wild rice,
mush, and milk to soothe
his stomach.
MINNESOTA HISTORICAL
SOCIETY.

River, the Coteau des Prairies, Big Stone Lake, and Lac qui
Parle, finally returning to Fort Snelling in mid-October.
This time, Featherstonhaugh was more comfortably
housed with Major Bliss and his family, and having a more
leisurely schedule, he visited the Pond brothers, the Indian
village at Lake Calhoun, and the Stephenses at Lake Harriet. He was entertained by the Taliaferros, the acting sutler,
and other officers—all but those of Major Loomis's "religious party." The major, said Featherstonaugh, "had not
even the decency to call upon me."

On October 22 in the midst of deep snow and bitter
cold, Featherstonhaugh and his party said goodbye to the
commandant and his officers at the fort. Across the river
at the fur-trading post, Featherstonhaugh said farewell to
Sibley and thanked him for his kindnesses and for the
invaluable services of Milor. The party then set off down

the Mississippi, the five voyageurs "singing at the tops of their fine voices" with now another passenger, John Bliss, Jr., who had been entrusted to Featherstonhaugh by his parents for delivery to Bliss family friends in the east.[49]

Sibley, perhaps exhibiting some patriotic and anti-British bias, and also taking exception to the explorer's unkind words about his friend Major Loomis, was not impressed by Featherstonhaugh. "His appearance and manners were ill calculated to ensure him a favorable reception among plain republicans. He was both autocratic and conceited. " His "productions" (writings) moreover, were "characterized by abuse of American society and of particular individuals." Others who encountered the visitor were also critical of his intolerant views on such subjects as tobacco, dirt, alcohol, and people of lesser social standing. Young John Bliss, who, with his parents, came to know Featherstonhaugh better than Sibley, called him "a large, fine looking and determined man, with many excellent qualities, but with an unfortunate disposition to bully and domineer over those who were under him."[50]

Down river at St. Louis, Featherstonhaugh met Joseph N. Nicollet, French astronomer, scientist, and explorer. Nicollet was fascinated by Featherstonhaugh's account of his adventures and there was "no doubt of Nicollet's desire to map the ground over which the Englishman had traveled." When the steamboat *St. Peters* came up river from St. Louis the next June, it brought Nicollet, who became one of Sibley's warm friends. Nicollet came with letters of introduction to Sibley, to military officers at the fort, and to Indian Agent Major Taliaferro. All welcomed him cordially and encouraged him as he developed his plans to travel first to the headwaters of the Mississippi. Taliaferro made available for his headquarters a small building near the Indian Agency. Sibley arranged for him to get from the sutler's store the supplies he would need for his expedition and helped him to find men who knew the region to go with him.[51]

When Nicollet returned at the end of September, his notebooks of observations were enough to keep him busy during the winter months drafting the map that was to be his crowning achievement. At times during the winter, he worked in his small headquarters, "wrapped in a bearskin, my head covered with a wool cap," to receive those who came to see him. At other times he crossed the river to stay with Sibley, spending "intense and unremitting" hours at work on his map. During evenings at Major Taliaferro's house, he played the violin accompanied by Mrs. Taliaferro on the piano, and at bedtime, Mrs. Taliaferro provided him a supper of wild rice, mush, and milk to soothe his stomach.

After an exploratory trip on the St. Croix the next summer, Nicollet left St. Peters and traveled to Washington, D.C., where he met Secretary of War Joel Poinsett, who was sufficiently impressed with Nicollet's work to arrange for funding his return west to gather additional materials for his map. He returned to St. Peters in 1838 and found a temporary home with Sibley, probably in his completed warehouse. There Nicollet and his assistants organized their outfit for an extended journey into the Dakota region. Among those assistants was Lieutenant John C. Fremont, who became Sibley's friend and hunting companion. Among all the visitors who stayed with Sibley at St. Peters, none appeared to be more agreeable than Nicollet and Lieutenant Fremont.[52]

Sibley's Sporting Life

Sibley was an enthusiastic sportsman. Many years after his first years at St. Peters, Sibley wrote that at that time "the bear, the deer, the fisher, the martin [marten], the amphibia, such as the mink and muskrat, were to be found in the streams and lakes, while the prairies were dotted with countless herds of bison and the elk, accompanied by their usual attendants, wolves and foxes, which scarcely deigned to seek concealment from the eye of the traveler. The numerous lakes and marshes were the breeding places of myriads of wild fowl, including swan, geese and ducks."[53]

Lion, one of Sibley's two huge Irish wolfhounds (the other was Boston), accompanied Sibley on his annual hunting adventures with the Dakota. This oil on canvas painting of Lion, commissioned by Sibley, was painted by Charles Deas in 1841, and now hangs in the Sibley House. MINNESOTA HISTORICAL SOCIETY.

This dramatic illustration of a buffalo hunt is from an 1853 eastern sporting publication, Guns and Shooting, *written in part by William T. Porter. Sibley not only enjoyed hunting firsthand but he liked to write about his adventures. His articles about life on the frontier, written under the pen name of Hal a Dakotah, were often published in Porter's publication, the* New York Spirit of the Times.

As soon as the weather permitted in the spring of 1835, Sibley shouldered his rifle and ventured out with Alexis Bailly for what he called "exercise and observation" on the banks of the St. Peters River. They had not gone far when they heard the honk of a gander and saw a flock of five geese. The men hid themselves in the bushes on the shore of a lake between the bluff and the river and imitated the call of the gander so successfully that the flock wheeled about and lighted "on the ice in the center of the lake, distant at least two hundred and fifty yards" from the two hunters.[54]

Sibley took aim at the head of the lead gander, "the bird fell with a heavy thud upon the frozen surface, and the rest of the flock took refuge in flight." How to retrieve the gander from the thawing ice was the next problem. "Snatching a pine board lying near the shore, Mr. Sibley started, in the face of his companion's protest, and made for the bird." He broke through several times "and after a long and fatiguing experience . . . [he] brought the game triumphantly to the dry land, at the cost of a complete immersion in the cold water." The fat goose provided a welcome meal for Sibley and the Baillys after their monotonous winter fare.

Sibley remembered another early-day spring duck-hunting adventure when he and an Indian were after the same flock. Both discharged their guns at the same time, killing eight fowl, the Indian shooting from a gun with one barrel, Sibley firing from a double-barreled shotgun. "With cool impudence, the Indian stepped to where eight fowls had fallen." One by one, he laced the heads of the ducks to his belt. Sibley was outraged and deliberately walking over to the Indian, removed each duck from the Indian's belt and attached it his own, "the Indian staring and mute with astonishment." Sibley then "held up *two* fingers, denoting that if he [the Indian] had been satisfied with *two* ducks, I would not have objected, but as he was so gluttonous as to appropriate the whole number, *he should have none.*" What the Indian made of this transaction is not known, but Sibley kept the ducks.

During the summer of 1835, Sibley went on a short excursion south to the Cannon River with Horatio N. Dillon, Major Taliaferro's brother-in-law, in search of lost muskrat traps. In the fall, he took a long-postponed trip to inspect his fur trading posts. In November 1835, after the season's work was completed and the Indians had gone on their winter hunt, he and two officer friends went out at last on his first extended hunting trip of the year.[55]

During the following years Sibley, prepared for more extensive hunting expeditions. He bought three horses from the Red River emigrants in 1835 and eventually acquired three more, having "six splendid horses, twenty-three of the finest dogs in all the region, six double-barreled shot-guns, three rifles, besides his holster pistols." On one expedition in 1840 he let his hair and beard grow and wore a buckskin hunting shirt and "light and pliable Indian moccasins." When he walked briskly through the woods in this attire, two enormous dogs at his heels, he encountered white men he knew well, but they did not recognize him, "wondering where such a wild man of the woods had come from."[56]

The huge dogs, two of his best, were Lion and Boston, "noble specimens of the Irish wolf dog, remarkable for their great size, and the indications not to be mistaken by practised eye of uncommon strength and speed." Lion was twenty-nine inches tall, more than five feet in length, and a very good watch dog. Sibley said it was not necessary to bolt his doors at night because Lion allowed no one to enter. In 1841 Sibley engaged a young artist, Charles Deas, to paint a life-size portrait of Lion, which hangs today in the Sibley House. Boston, about an inch shorter, and a hound "of indomitable courage and fierceness hesitating not when roused to attack," was given to Sibley by Captain Martin Scott, who had served with the Fifth Infantry at Fort Snelling in the 1820s and returned with his regiment in the summer of 1837. Scott was known far and wide as one of the best shots and keenest sportsmen in the country and soon became one of Sibley's favorite hunting companions.[57]

Either Scott or friends at Detroit or Green Bay may

have helped Sibley to find Lion and he seems to have had both dogs before the winter of 1838. Described more precisely as half Irish wolfhound and half Scottish greyhound (or deerhound), Lion and Boston were unusual dogs to be found on the Minnesota frontier at this time. The two breeds in Scotland and Ireland were the hunting companions and exclusive property of the ruling classes. They were bred to the chase, and there is mention of these "swift hounds" of the Celts as early as 273 B.C. As a result of political upheaval and the disappearance of big game, few of these animals remained by the early nineteenth century. But both breeds were restored and standards set for them during the later 1800s.[58]

With a number of his fur trade employees, Joseph Jack Frazer (whose biography Sibley later wrote), and Lieutenant Fremont, Sibley and his dogs accompanied a band of Indians on a winter hunting expedition south and west toward the Des Moines River. He was away from home for some seventy days. On another such expedition, he was absent from St. Peters from October 1 to the end of January. He estimated that in that period, "more than 2,000 deer, 50 or 60 elk, many bears, and a few buffaloes had been destroyed," as well as five or six panthers.[59]

By 1846 Sibley had become a regular contributor to the New York outdoor publication *The Spirit of the Times*, writing under the pen name of *Hal a Dakotah* about "life on the frontier, Indian character and warfare, and sporting incidents and adventures." An anthology of 1853 contained two of Sibley's contributions, "Hunting on the Western Prairies," describing expeditions in present-day Iowa, and "Buffalo Hunting," which described a twenty-two-day excursion in the Dakota region in 1842. When Sibley and his companions returned home that year they

Joseph Jack Frazer, or Iron Face, a man of Dakota-Scottish ancestry, was an employee of Sibley's and a frequent companion on hunting expeditions.
MINNESOTA HISTORICAL SOCIETY.

had, "in the interval, killed sixteen buffalo, three elk, eight raccoons, twelve wolves, seven geese, two hundred and forty-four ducks, and eighty grouse, besides sundry other snaps not worth recording."[60]

While Sibley recorded times when the Indians slaughtered only the animals they could use, more often he noted without criticism, as he did here, the totals of the kill. By the 1850s, however, he could see that the wild game had been killed off in great numbers and their remnants driven father west. He criticized all who indulged in this slaughter and came to see the need for legislation that would "avoid the total extinction of both animals and wild fowl."[61]

As big game became more scarce in the 1850s, hunting became less pleasurable. Sibley remembered and wrote about his earlier outdoor adventures, but his changing life style gave him less time for sports and the chase.

I believe that my fondness for hunting kept me from becoming demoralized by the temptations which surrounded every man in the Indian trade at that time, and were the ruin of many. With plenty of leisure on their hands during portions of the year, unrestrained by the ties of family or refined society they were too apt to give up their time to gambling, to the bowl, or to vicious indulgences which the proximity of the wigwam will suggest. But my fondness for shooting kept me out of such temptations. When not actually engaged in business I was out with my guns and dogs in pursuit of game, and this being a sort of passion with me, kept any other inclination from taking hold of me.[62]

Henry H. Sibley, *Unfinished Autobiography*

Sibley's Later Years

In 1837 the U.S. government negotiated treaties with the Ojibwe and Dakota Indians that opened large areas of their lands to white settlement. The Ojibwe treaty was negotiated at Fort Snelling and there Sibley would have met young Franklin Steele, who had come west from Pennsylvania in search of his fortune. Steele invested at first in the St. Croix Lumber Company, a business concerned with exploiting the rich white pine lands of the upper St. Croix River. Later he was to succeed Sibley as sutler at Fort Snelling and to be associated with the development of the water power at St. Anthony Falls. The Dakota treaty, negotiated in September 1837 in Washington, D.C., was of more direct interest to Sibley, and he traveled there to do what he could to advance the Company's interests.[63]

In Washington again a few years later on Company business, he found time to attend his friend Franklin Steele's wedding and meet Steele's young sister, Sarah Jane. The two became better acquainted when she came with her brother and his wife to Fort Snelling. Sibley spent many hours courting Sarah Jane during the winter of 1842–43 and the two were married in May 1843, when Sibley was thirty two.[64]

Mrs. Sibley's arrival as mistress of the stone house at St. Peters presaged major changes in Sibley's bachelor household. His dog Lion, for example, accustomed to the run of the house, was not willing to share quarters with the new mistress and moved out, finding a new home across the river at Fort Snelling. He is said to have lived there the rest of his life. While Lion was pleased to see Sibley when his

Sarah Steele Sibley, as she looked in a daguerreotype from the 1850s.

old master visited the fort, he never returned to his Mendota home and apparently never hunted with Sibley again.

Changes in the fur trade business occurred in the next decade when Sibley's Sioux Outfit became a part of the St. Louis firm of Pierre Chouteau Jr. and Company and then in 1853, when Sibley ended his connection with the fur trade. When settlers moved onto the former Indian lands, Sibley began to invest in lands and townsites.

As one who had come to know his way around Washington, Sibley was a logical person to represent the settlers of the growing communities who wanted to organize as a territory. He was chosen a new delegate from Wisconsin Territory to the Thirtieth Congress, where he was influential in the organization of the new Minnesota Territory,

Henry Sibley as he looked in 1870 when he was in his 60s.
MINNESOTA HISTORICAL SOCIETY.

the drawing of its boundaries, the choice of its name, and the designation of its capital, St. Paul. When Minnesota became a state, he served on the Democratic branch of the state's bifurcated constitutional convention and, in 1858, was elected Minnesota's first state governor.

Sibley and his family lived on at St. Peters, which by the 1840s became known as Mendota. In 1862 they moved to a new home in St. Paul and in the same year Governor Alexander Ramsey called on Sibley to command the volunteers against the Dakota, who had attacked white farms and settlements on the Minnesota frontier. Sibley was subsequently appointed to head the army's Military District of Minnesota, and his military service continued until the end of the Civil War.

When Sibley was away from home during the war two of his young children died; of the couple's nine children, only four lived beyond childhood. Those who survived were Augusta, the eldest, Sara Jane, Charles Frederick, and Alfred Brush. In 1869 Mrs. Sibley died; her youngest child was only two years old.

Sibley never remarried, but his wife's sister Abby (Mrs. Thomas) Potts kept house for him and his family. His business interests after the war were as an officer of the St. Paul gas company; his community activities were with the Minnesota Historical Society and the St. Paul Chamber of Commerce; but he continued to be interested in the welfare of the Indians and helped to negotiate treaties with them. He served the state in a project for the relief of settlers suffering from grasshopper infestations, and he was selected a regent of the University of Minnesota.

Sibley's home in his tranquil later years was a pleasant place set in the midst of wooded lots on Woodward Avenue, just east of downtown St. Paul. In his household were Mrs. Potts (now a widow) and her son, Charles; Sibley's widowed eldest daughter Augusta (Mrs. Douglas) Pope and her three daughters; and Alfred, Sibley's youngest son.[65]

Each morning, six days a week, it was his custom to go downtown to his office in the Globe Building, driven by his Swedish servant, John, in a "modest vehicle," behind an "old but grand 'white horse.'"

In the early afternoon he returned to his home and, after a nap, the gray-bearded Sibley, stouter than he had once been, "gold spectacles adjusted to a proper position," reclined in a comfortable chair in his sitting room, reading, entertaining his friends, or enjoying the society of his children and grandchildren. On the wall behind his chair was the Charles Deas painting of his dog, Lion, and an oil painting of Mendota in 1836. At times, he wrote memoirs of his own early days and biographical sketches of some of the pioneers he had known for the Historical Society's collections.[66] In 1891, in these quiet surroundings, Henry H. Sibley died, in his eightieth year.

Notes

1. The description of Sibley's early years before going to St. Peters is taken from the following sources: *The Unfinished Autobiography of Henry Hastings Sibley, Together with a Selection of Hitherto Unpublished Letters from the Thirties,* ed. Theodore C. Blegen, 7–29 (Minneapolis, 1932) (the original manuscript of which is in the Henry Hastings Sibley Papers in the Minnesota Historical Society [hereafter MHS] and on roll 32 of the microfilm edition of those papers); Jane Spector Davis, *Guide to a Microfilm Edition of the Henry Hastings Sibley Papers,* 2, 7 (St. Paul, 1968); and J. Fletcher Williams, "Henry Hastings Sibley, A Memoir," in *Minnesota Historical Collections* (hereafter cited as *MHC*) 6:257–64 (St. Paul, 1894).
2. The quotation is from William Watts Folwell, *A History of Minnesota,* 1:161 (Revised edition, St. Paul, 1956). For more on Fort Brady, see Otto Fowle, *Sault Ste. Marie and Its Great Waterway,* 326–34 (New York, 1925).
3. Rhoda R. Gilman, "Last Days of the Upper Mississippi Fur Trade," *Minnesota History* (hereafter cited as *MH*) 42 (Winter 1970):123–26.
4. Williams, "Sibley Memoir," *MHC* 6:268.
5. Here and next paragraphs, see Sibley, *Unfinished Autobiography,* 24–26; Williams, "Sibley Memoir," *MHC* 6:262.
6. For details of the journey, see Sibley, *Unfinished Autobiography,* 26–30; H. H. Sibley, "Reminiscences of the Early Days of Minnesota," *MHC* 3:245 (St. Paul, 1880); Nathaniel West, *The Ancestry, Life, and Times of Hon. Henry Hastings Sibley, LL.D,* 55–56 (St. Paul, 1889). Mendota, a Sioux (Dakota) name for the site at the mouth of the St. Peters or Minnesota River, became the name of the community where Sibley lived; see Warren Upham, *Minnesota Geographic Names, MHC* 17:166 (St. Paul, 1920).
7. Here and below, see Sibley, *Unfinished Autobiography,* 29–30, and in the same source, Sibley to Ramsay Crooks, November 1, 1834, p. 47–49.
8. Sibley to Mrs. Solomon Sibley, August 1, 1835, Burton Historical Collection, roll 1:338–39, Sibley Papers.
9. Sibley, *Unfinished Autobiography,* 35.
10. Helen White and Bruce M. White, "Fort Snelling in 1838," 151–54 (St. Paul, 1998), copy in MHS Historic Sites Department.
11. West, *Ancestry, Life and Times,* 418.
12. Here and in the next two paragraphs, see *The Sibley Historic Site,* 6 (Mendota, 1995).
13. Here and below, see Sibley, "Reminiscences," *MHC* 3:247–48, 250. The names of the Dakota Indian bands are spelled here as in Folwell, *Minnesota,* 1:182–83.
14. Sibley, "Reminiscences," *MHC* 3:246.
15. Sibley, "Reminiscences," *MHC* 3:267, 320; West, *Ancestry, Life, and Times,* 67–68.
16. Alan R. Woolworth, "Helen Hastings Sibley, 1841–1860," manuscript (in the possession of the author) that summarizes his own research and that

of other scholars concerning Sibley's daughter, Helen Hastings Sibley. Their evidence supports a birth date (1841) and lineage different from those given in Davis, *Guide*, 3. See also Helen Hastings Sibley Sawyer to William R. Brown, December 8, 1859, William R. Brown Papers, MHS, and "House and its Heroine," *St. Paul Sunday Dispatch*, October 25, 1908; "The Story of Nancy McClure," *MHC* 6:438–60.

17. Here and below, see Sibley, *Unfinished Autobiography*, 38–39.

18. Marcus Hansen, *Old Fort Snelling, 1819–1858,* 77–79 (Iowa City, 1918); White and White, "Fort Snelling in 1838," 81–87. See also the map of Lt. Ephraim K. Smith, 1837, reproduced in this booklet.

19. Here and below, see Colonel John H. Bliss, "Reminiscences of Fort Snelling," *MHC* 6:335–53 (St. Paul, 1894); Sibley, *Unfinished Autobiography*, 30–32. It should be noted that Sibley's memories of the winter of 1834–35 cannot be relied on in some details; for example, the First Infantry was in residence at the fort that year; his friends the Loomises, Ogden, and McClure were all members of the First; the Fifth, with Major Joseph Plympton and Captain Martin Scott, did not come until 1837 (Francis B. Heitman, *Historical Register and Dictionary of the United States Army*, 641, 658, 757 and *MHC* 1:358–59).

20. Samuel W. Pond, "The Dakota or Sioux in Minnesota as They Were in 1834," *MHC* 12:341 (St. Paul, 1908).

21. Here and the next two paragraphs, see Nathan S. Jarvis to William Jarvis, December 31, 1834, in Nathan S. Jarvis Papers (originals in the New York Academy of Medicine, New York City, copies at MHS). The term "kickshaws," a corruption of the French *quelque chose,* according to Noah Webster's *First Edition of An American Dictionary of the English Language* (1828; 11th printing facsimile edition, San Francisco, 1995), means "Something fantastical or uncommon or something that has no particular name," or "A dish so changed by cooking that it can scarcely be known."

22. In his letter to Sibley of March 27, 1828, Robert A. [Kinzie] mentions that he has heard that Sibley was a member of the Thespian Society at Detroit; roll 1:189–92, Sibley Papers.

23. Records Sibley kept for the Fort Snelling sutler store include nineteen account books (vols. 70–88) filmed on rolls 27–28, Sibley Papers; Francis Paul Prucha, "Army Sutlers and the American Fur Company," *MH* 40 (Spring 1966):22–31; Sibley, *Unfinished Autobiography*, 51, 60–61, 65, 68.

24. For the Thespian accounts, see vols. 87 and 88, roll 28, Sibley Papers.

25. Among the items relating to Baker's accounts as sutler in the Kenneth Mackenzie Papers, Missouri Historical Society, are statements of September 9, 1838, and January 3 and April 16, 1840; see also Helen M. White, "Benjamin F. Baker Chronology," manuscript in the possession of the author.

26. Here and below, see Sibley to Mrs. Solomon Sibley, August 1, 1835, roll 1:338–39, and Taliaferro to Sibley, December 8, 1835, roll 1:376, Sibley Papers; Lawrence Taliaferro Journal, August 28, 1835, Taliaferro Papers, MHS. Citations to the Taliaferro Papers are given here only by date from the typewritten transcript; the originals are copied in the microfilm edi-

tion, Helen M. White, editor, *A Microfilm Edition of the Lawrence Talia-ferro Papers* (St. Paul, 1966).

27. Frederick and Elizabeth Ayer to Sibley, May 2, 1835, Sibley Papers, roll 1:306. For Richard F. Cadle, see Elizabeth Therese Baird, "Reminis-cences of Life in Territorial Wisconsin, 1824–1842," *Wisconsin Historical Collections*, 15:222–24 (Madison, 1900). For an amusing incident of Sib-ley's Sabbath observance, see Sibley, "Reminiscences," *MHC* 3:264.

28. Theodore C. Blegen, "The Pond Brothers," *MH* 15:273 (1934).

29. Samuel W. Pond, "The Cabin by the Lake or the Story of Two Pioneers," 26:46, Pond Papers, MHS.

30. Here and below, see Samuel Pond to Herman Hine, January 19, 1835, Pond Papers.

31. Here and below, see Samuel Pond, "The Cabin by the Lake," 26:45– 47½, Pond Papers.

32. Here and below, see Gideon to Ruth Pond, November 2, 14, 1834, Pond Papers.

33. Samuel W. Pond, "Review of Life and Personal Recollections," 25:97, and Gideon to Ruth Pond, November 2 and 14, 1834, all in Pond Papers.

34. Samuel Pond, "The Cabin by the Lake," 26:74, Pond Papers.

35. Samuel Pond, "The Cabin by the Lake," 26:78; Samuel W. Pond to Her-man Hine, January 19, 1835, and to Mrs. Sarah Pond, September 2, 1835, and Gideon Pond to Jared Frost, February 23, 1835, all in Pond Papers.

36. Folwell, *Minnesota* 1:189–207; Hansen, *Fort Snelling*, 154–58; West, *Ancestry, Life, and Times*, 90.

37. Albert B. Marshall, *History of the First Presbyterian Church of Minneapolis, Minnesota, 1835–1910*, 19–21 (Minneapolis, 1910).

38. Sibley, "Reminiscences," *MHC* 3:269–70.

39. Henry H. Sibley, "Buffalo Hunting," Peter Hawker and William T. Porter, *Instructions to Young Sportsmen in All that Relates to Guns and Shooting*, 271 (Philadelphia, 1853).

40. Sibley to J. Fletcher Williams, April 16, 1877, in Williams, "Sibley Mem-oir," *MHC* 6:304.

41. Sibley, *Unfinished Autobiography*, 35.

42. Taliaferro Journal, June 29, 1835; George Catlin, *Illustrations of the Man-ners, Customs, and Condition of the North American Indians* (London, 1845, fifth edition). Catlin's plates numbered 131–35, 276–79, and 320–24 are of particular interest for this text. Sibley apparently first saw Catlin's letters and notes in Eastern newspapers.

43. Here and below, Sibley, "Reminiscences: Historical and Personal," *MHC* 1:393.

44. Jarvis to William Jarvis, August 2, 1835, Jarvis Papers; Mrs. Ann Adams, "Early Days at Red River Settlement," *MHC* 6:89. Adams and her family came with twelve other Swiss emigrant families of Red River people to Fort Snelling in 1823. By 1835 Taliaferro counted 489 Red River emi-grants (Taliaferro Journal, July 31 and August 3–4; Hansen, *Fort Snel-ling*, 188–90).

45. Jarvis to William Jarvis, August 2, 1835, Jarvis Papers; Taliaferro Journal, October 10, 1835.

46. George Featherstonhaugh, *A Canoe Voyage up the Minnay Sotor* 1:158 (reprint edition, St. Paul, 1970); Sibley, *Unfinished Autobiography*, 32–33; West, *Ancestry, Life and Times*, 91. Featherstonhaugh's "Report of a Geological Reconnaisance," without personal details, was printed in 1835 as 24 Congress, *Senate Executive Document* 333, serial 282.

47. Featherstonhaugh's experiences at Fort Snelling, here and below, are described in *A Canoe Voyage*, 1:258–83.

48. Featherstonhaugh, *A Canoe Voyage,* 1:259; Sibley, *Unfinished Autobiography*, 33–34.

49. Bliss, "Reminiscences," *MHC* 5:351; Featherstonhaugh, *A Canoe Voyage,* 2:15.

50. Sibley, "Reminiscences: Historical and Personal," *MHC* 3:393; Bliss, "Reminiscences," *MHC* 6:352.

51. Here and below, see Martha Coleman Bray, ed., *The Journals of Joseph N. Nicollet,* 9, 15, 23–27 (St. Paul, 1970); and Martha Coleman Bray, *Joseph Nicollet and His Map,* 6–8 (Philadelphia, 2d ed., 1994).

52. Sibley, *Unfinished Autobiography*, 35; *The Expeditions of John Charles Fremont,* eds. Donald Jackson and Mary Lee Spence, 1:10–21 (Urbana, Ill., 1970).

53. Sibley, *Unfinished Autobiography*, 32–33.

54. For two versions of these exploits, here and below, see Sibley, *Unfinished Autobiography*, 32–34; West, *Ancestry, Life, and Times*, 56–59.

55. Taliaferro Journal, August 13, October 7, 28, and November 6, 1835; Sibley, *Unifinished Autobiography*, 36–38.

56. Taliaferro Journal, July 31, 1835; Sibley, "Hunting in the Western Prairies," in Hawker and Porter, *Instructions to Young Sportsmen*, 393–94; Williams, "Sibley, Memoir," *MHC* 6:272; West, *Ancestry, Life, and Times*, 78, 424.

57. Sibley, "Hunting in the Western Prairies," in Hawker and Porter, *Instructions to Young Sportsmen*, 393–94; West, *Ancestry Life and Times*, 421. On Scott, see Heitman, *Historical Register*, 869, and Williams, "Sibley Memoir," *MHC* 6:272; for Deas, the artist whose brother was an officer of the Fifth Infantry stationed at Fort Crawford, see *M. and M. Karolik Collection of American Paintings, 1815–1865,* 212–14 (Cambridge, Mass., 1949).

58. [Helen M. White], "Rare Hound," 8, *Sibley House Visitor* (1972); see also Joel Samaha, *The New Complete Irish Wolfhound,* 29, 194–97, 221 (on Scottish deerhound) (New York: Howell Book House, n.d.). The author states that Sibley imported Irish wolfhounds Lion and Tiger from England—the first "recorded" in America. Tiger is said to have been ferocious and had to be destroyed; Jay Edgerton, "Henry Sibley Wed, and His Dog Fled," *Minneapolis Star,* August 18, 1956, 7A. Sibley speaks only of Lion and Boston in Hawker and Porter, *Instructions to Young Sportsmen*, 394; and in Sibley to Fred Sibley, April 21, 1839, Burton Historical Collection, roll 2:249, Sibley Papers, he says that Lion was half Irish wolfhound and half "Scotch greyhound." He also writes about his dogs in letters to Solomon Sibley, September 26, 1838, and December 16, 1839.

59. Sibley, "Reminiscences," *MHC* 3:255–57; Theodore C. Blegen and Sarah J. Davidson, eds, *Iron Face: The Adventures of Jack Frazer* (Chicago, 1950).

60. John T. Flanagan, "Big Game Hunter, Henry H. Sibley," *MH* 41 (Spring 1969):217–28, 226–27; Sibley, "Buffalo Hunting," 265–73, and "Hunting in the Western Prairies," 393–423, in Hawker and Porter, *Instructions to Young Sportsmen*.

61. Flanagan, "Big Game Hunter," *MH* 41:228.

62. Williams, "Sibley Memoir," *MHC* 6:271.

63. Here and below, see Davis, *Guide to the Sibley Papers,* 3–5, 14–21.

64. David M. Grabitske, "Sarah Jane: A Lady's Frontier in Minnesota," 20–32, *Open Air Museums,* 20:3 (1999).

65. Here and in the next two paragraphs, see West, *Ancestry, Life, and Times,* 420-21, 425-27; Williams, "Sibley Memoir," *MHC* 6:275, 306.

66. The painting said to be of Mendota in 1836 could be one of several done by Edward K. Thomas, such as the one on the cover of this book. Although Thomas painted around 1850, he appears to have emphasized the primitive aspects of the scene. Sibley continued in old age to be interested in the Minnesota Historical Society, and after his death his family gave his business records and much of his correspondence to the Society. His papers became one of the Society's collections of national significance as an important source of information on Indians affairs and the fur trade of the Upper Mississippi Valley, as well as on the settlement, politics, and economic development of early Minnesota. Copied on microfilm in an edition sponsored by the National Historical Publications Commission, his papers have been made available nationwide to all who are interested in studying Sibley's life and times. They were a major source of information for this book. See Helen M. White, "Introduction," in Davis, *Guide to the Sibley Papers,* [n.p.].

ABOUT THE AUTHOR: Helen M. White's history with Henry H. Sibley and Fort Snelling goes back more than 40 years. Her work from 1961 to 1970 as special research historian at the Minnesota Historical Society provided much of the information used for the restoration of Fort Snelling. Nearly 30 years later, in 1998, she and co-author Bruce White researched and wrote "Fort Snelling in 1838: An Ethnographic and Historical Study," a report prepared for the MHS Historic Sites Department. Working as Assistant and Associate Curator of Manuscripts for the MHS, White became well acquainted with Sibley and many other 19th-century Minnesotans who helped shape and guide the state in its early years. She was director and editor of the National Historical Publications Commission projects to microfilm the records and papers of Sibley, Taliaferro, James W. Taylor, and Alexander Ramsey, and she wrote the guides to the Donnelly, Taliaferro, and Ramsey Papers. Her published books include *A Small Yellow House* (Beaver's Pond Press, 2001), an account of her restoration of an 1857 house in Taylors Falls; *The Tale of a Comet* (MHS Press, 1984), and *Ho! For the Gold Fields* (MHS Press, 1966), which received an Award of Merit from the American Association for State and Local History.